LEADERSHIP:

LESSON ONE

Leadership: Lesson One
Morten Heedegaard

First edition

ISBN   978-87-998856-0-2

Editing: Beverley Lennox

Formatting: DIY Publishing Ltd

Cover: Mila Perry, CreativeMotions

Print: CreateSpace

www.lesson.one

LEADERSHIP: LESSON ONE

The right results tomorrow require
effective leadership today.

Effective leadership requires the right skills.

LEADERSHIP: LESSON ONE provides the
foundation for building effective
leadership skills.

Morten Heedegaard

CONTENTS

PREFACE

Here you are—sitting in a leadership position because someone has great confidence in you—your manager.

Promoting you into that leadership position—whether it is your first leadership position or a more senior position—comes with an obligation on the part of your manager to offer you the support you need to grow and become a successful leader. And, likewise, you have the same responsibility for your team.

Most leaders are appointed into their first leadership roles based on their technical expertise. And, in many cases, this happens suddenly, and implies a massive change for new leaders.

While LEADERSHIP: LESSON ONE is a useful guide for freshly minted leaders, it can also provide value to more seasoned leaders. When you get bogged down in complex projects, the simple framework in LEADERSHIP: LESSON ONE will help you get things back on track. And if you have just appointed new leaders to your team, it is a useful guide to help you coach them and increase their competencies so that they too can lead with confidence.

The objective of the framework is to help you produce results, as that is ultimately what matters. I am not a proponent of results at any expense, and the framework takes that into account by integrating the importance of developing people's capabilities along the way.

In the game of tennis, you have to have the right grip on the pracket before you can go on to master the game. Much like tennis, leaders need to grasp some core concepts before they can master the subtle nuances of leadership. The core concepts are the foundation upon which they can add more complex layers. But the core remains the same, and they can return to it time and time again to set them on the right path.

Leaders are an essential part of any organization; they set direction, motivate others and shape results. Whether they are senior leaders in a large multinational, team leaders or junior project managers, they have all been new to leadership at some point, and they all need to grasp some core concepts in order to lead with confidence.

During my first appointment to a leadership role more than 15 years ago, I was feeling frustrated and had a lot of questions: What is leadership all about? Where is the instruction manual? How do I lead? And, how is my success as a leader measured? Overnight, I made the transition from being an "expert in my field" to suddenly being thrust into a leadership role. I was no longer required to complete tasks and projects; instead, I had to lead others. This was a completely new game, and it shook my self-confidence.

Several years later, I came to realize that my continuous search for *the right way to lead* was a never-ending journey. So I redirected my energy into finding the simple, core components that could apply to any leadership situation.

Since I have always enjoyed understanding how things work and condensing problems down to their essence, I decided to set my sights on unravelling the leadership puzzle.

When I stand back and look at the various projects and tasks I have been responsible for over the past 10+ years, I see that I had some hits and some misses along the way.

The interesting thing is that the misses offered the most learning. As I dug deeper into the reasons why my objectives were not met, it came down to one or some combination of four root causes. Nothing more, nothing less. Just four.

When I turned this around, and looked at my hits, it appeared that all four of these components were in good shape.

Once you condense it down to the four powerful, yet simple components that are at the core of leadership, you can then begin to add more complex layers, but the four core components remain the same.

The simple framework outlined in this book serves as a solid base for continuous growth. When things feel out of control, you can always return to the core components. They will help you shape your day-to-day interactions with both your superiors and your team.

LEADERSHIP: LESSON ONE is dedicated to leaders and managers who dare to look in the mirror and reflect on ways in which they can improve their leadership skills to produce better results.

And therefore it only adds value when you start practicing—and thereby grow your leadership in a direction that also includes the continuous development of your team or the people you are working with.

As long as you can identify with the belief that continuously strengthening the basics is a great way for you to grow, I hope you will benefit from this simple, yet powerful framework.

Introduction: The Footprint of a Leader

The terms management and leadership are often used interchangeably. While they are related, they are very different.

Leadership is the role of defining a vision or future direction, while *Management* implies steering within a given set of frameworks, objectives, processes or structures. In other words, the leader sets the destination; the manager makes sure you arrive.

Oftentimes, the leader and manager roles are held by the same person. And this book takes that into account because you cannot manage without leadership, and if you try to lead without managing, your impact will be limited.

To avoid confusion, I generally use leadership when referring to these roles.

Eventually, as a leader, we all leave our positions. When that happens, there are two types of footprints in the sand that we can make before we leave: big, bold and long lasting or small, weak and quickly gone.

Ultimately, you want your footprint to contain two elements:

1. Achieve results today to leave a big, bold footprint.
2. Develop people to take on tomorrow and leave a long-lasting footprint.

Together, these two achievements are the ultimate characteristics of a good leader. If you can develop people to continue achieving solid results even after you are gone, you have done your job.

Achieving solid results needs no further explanation—it is mandatory. However, ensuring that people develop and grow is also vital, though it is easily overlooked in the day-to-day quest for short-term results.

The rate of change has accelerated to the point where the competencies required five years ago are no longer enough today. As a result, it is critical to continuously develop the relevant skills and competencies that will be required not only today, but also in the future.

**Today's results arose
from yesterday's competencies.**

And tomorrow's results will depend on your ability to grow competencies today.

If you fail to achieve results, you typically will not last long in your job. However, achieving results without developing people often goes unnoticed in the short term, but it results in an unsustainable situation for the organization. Without a competent workforce, an organization cannot survive.

If, however, you have focused on developing people and growing their competencies, but you are not achieving results in the short or medium term, you will not last long either.

Great leaders do not result from a single event or leadership program; they evolve over time, and their skill level is the culmination of a variety of events and experiences.

If you look at an organization today, you see a *current state* that reflects the past decisions leaders have made, or not made, within the organization to optimize the future. It also reflects the competencies within the organization, and to some extent, those external factors that have come into play that were beyond anyone's control.

And in all cases, the fact remains that without the combination of strong leadership and a competent team, even the best leaders will have difficulty driving results. Both are essential. And, it will take time for both to grow and evolve. As Vincent van Gogh once said:

**Great things are not done by impulse,
but by a series
of small things brought together.**

Random courses and seminars every now and then are not enough to develop the competencies required across an entire organization; nor are they enough to develop a strong leader. Like exercise, a couple of weeks a year does not make you physically fit.

Training needs to be integrated into regular work. You do not need to tack it onto your already busy workweek. Instead, you need to integrate what you know into *how* you lead and practice it every day. And growing competencies is a big part of the leadership DNA.

This requires you, as the leader, to evaluate the strengths and weaknesses of your team members on an ongoing basis. Rather than waiting for their annual or semi-annual performance reviews, you must provide them with more timely feedback. Next, you need to work with them to find ways to grow their competencies.

Training sessions can play a role, but they provide the most value when they are linked back to their daily tasks, which again are linked to the overall goals and future requirements of your team and the entire organization.

LEADERSHIP: LESSON ONE views both strong results and the development of competencies as an integrated whole—they are both equally important.

What then are the limits of a leader's responsibility?

Ultimately, there are no limits. In the end, the leader remains responsible.

The leader has a mandate to not only hire people, but also fire them, or propose organizational changes to a superior, if their performance is not good enough. Furthermore, the leader has the right as well as the obligation to anchor areas of responsibility within the team.

Accountability for results ultimately rests on the shoulders of the leader. When the progress of a project team or direct report is poor, it is ultimately the responsibility of the leader. And when results are delivered, or if they exceed expectations, the true leader directs the gratitude and applause towards the team.

**True leaders take the blame;
the team takes the fame.**

When an organizational initiative fails to achieve its objective, you can usually link it back to the decisions that were made, or not made, the execution or external factors that were not addressed. At the end of the day, it is the leader who is responsible for the decisions that were made, or perhaps more importantly, the decisions that were *not* made.

Mistakes can be a fantastic source of learning, when used constructively to consider what went wrong, what could have been done differently and—ultimately—what was learned.

Daring to discuss failure through a learning lens is a crucial step in adopting better ways of working and ultimately growing the leader and team's ability to be more proactive when necessary. Often, with just a slight shift by the leader at an earlier stage, the team can make more progress. If we admit that the leader is not always right, we give ourselves an excellent opportunity to learn!

Some cultures have little tolerance for failures, which, in turn, may stifle creativity and encourage risk avoidance. Yet in other cultures, people are tolerant of mistakes.

The best culture is a culture where people are *obliged to learn* from the mistakes that undoubtedly will happen.

A true leader never lets the learning stop, whether it is his or her learning or the team's learning.

LESSON ONE

LEADERSHIP: LESSON ONE is a way of looking at a business, team, organization, project or task through a window of two fundamental questions:

1. WHAT? What do you want to achieve?
2. HOW? How will you do it?

WHAT and HOW will remain central themes throughout the rest of the book.

The process starts with you, as the leader, thinking and reflecting on a leadership challenge: A task, a project or a change you need to make or adapt to eventually. If the challenge is something new, or if you are feeling frustrated in the middle of an initiative, start by asking yourself, "What is the destination?" and "How will I get there?"

In reality, lack of progress is seldom traced back to just WHAT or HOW. Very often, it is a combination of both. To succeed, there needs to be the right balance between WHAT and HOW because they are closely linked, and your end result will only be as strong as the weakest link.

If you are experiencing a lack of progress, not meeting your results or milestones or things are moving too slowly, it almost always originates with the decisions you have made with regard to WHAT and HOW.

The methodology outlined in this book can be used on a day-to-day basis as a guiding framework for your leadership as well as on a larger scale to kick off new initiatives. It will help you foresee and continuously adjust the right elements during various phases of a project. And it will help you motivate and align your team with your objectives. You can apply it to situations that are working well as well as those that need improvement.

Importantly, rather than just using it as a post-mortem approach, it can be used as a proactive way of thinking that is based on a journey of learning and reflection, whereby you are continuously striving to find better ways of doing things, i.e. you are constantly calibrating, adapting, learning and adjusting.

WHAT? and HOW?—are the central components of LEADERSHIP: LESSON ONE. In the coming sections, we will look more closely at the underlying elements of WHAT and How to understand how to use them to make and implement the best decisions for success.

To maximize the benefit you derive from this book, apply what you learn from the remainder of the book to an actual situation, task or project that you are facing.

WHAT DO YOU WANT TO ACHIEVE?

WHAT is the objective of the task, project or organization?

WHAT involves understanding where you are heading. To get there, you must close the gap between where you are today and where you want to go—your goal or desired future state (*refer to **Figure 1***). This journey starts with a vision that outlines the dream you want to achieve, the objective you want to meet or the direction you want to go in.

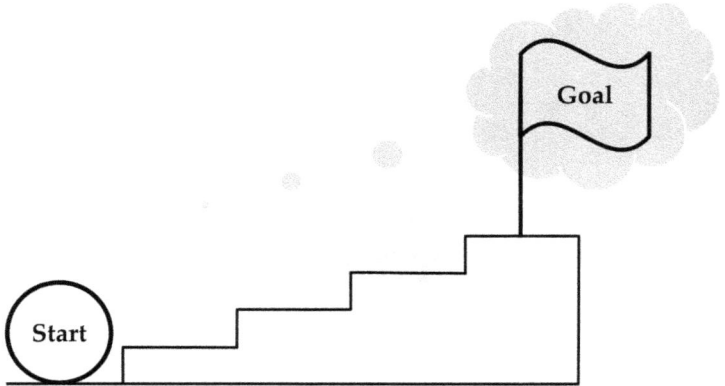

Figure 1: WHAT does success look like?

WHAT is the first element of the leadership journey. It starts with you as the leader, and at some point, you must also involve your team.

YOUR WHAT

The first part of WHAT is all about you—the leader—shaping your own vision of what you want to achieve, what results you want to deliver. As discussed in the "The Footprint of a Leader" section, leaders are crucial for driving results in organizations, and for those results to be realized, the leader needs to understand and own the vision.

Formulating an idea of a future direction or goal on an individual basis is a crucial first step as it sets the scene for the remainder of the journey.

If you do not know where you want to go, you can never convince a team to join you on the journey.

Depending on the situation you are facing, the WHAT can be very clear and measurable, or, rather than specific, it can be more directional as follows:

- Grow our customer base.

- Increase our production efficiency.

- Get previous month's results sooner.

- Ensure success of our new product.

- Lower our stock levels.

If your initial target—your WHAT—seems a little vague like the above examples, that is OK. They indicate a direction, rather than specify exactly what you aim to achieve. At this point it is your instincts telling you that you still need to do some work on shaping it further to make it more specific, which in itself is an important insight.

Whether it is a clear vision or more directional in nature, it is the starting point of the leadership journey to drive change and improve performance.

Take a moment to reflect:

Can you clearly, without overthinking, state the ultimate WHAT for your most important task right now?

Unless you have your own business and you are your own boss, you probably have a leader—your manager. Your manager is, of course, your first important source of input to help sharpen your WHAT. Your directional targets may even come from him or her. In fact, a solid, mutual understanding between you and your manager about your success criteria is critical, and it is also critical when leading a team or a project. If you do not know how your success will be measured, you cannot help your team achieve success in the eyes of your manager.

To define the WHAT more clearly, one can take various routes. You can translate your directional objectives into more specific targets by yourself, perhaps with input from your peers in the organization. Or, you can involve your team.

Involving the team at an early stage, helps build the team's commitment because it has contributed to shaping the targets.

If you have a current project or task, where the WHAT is not yet fully defined, think about who could support you in shaping it.

Sometimes, the process of getting from "something needs to be done" to the point where you know exactly WHAT you are aiming for can be an iterative process (*refer to **Figure 2***). You may have some sort of direction in mind, but you need input from others to sharpen your vision. Several iterations may be required to get the details you need that will bring clarity to the point where WHAT is no longer a question; it is a concrete objective.

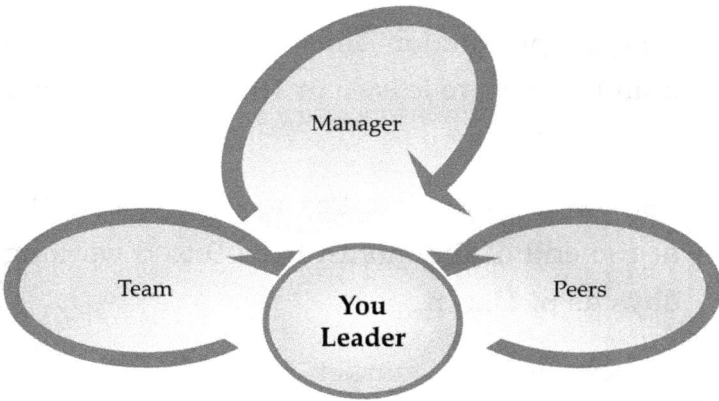

Figure 2: Seeking input to refine WHAT

In the end, you will help shape your WHAT into very clear objectives that build on the initial vision or idea of what it is you want to achieve, for example:

- Acquire 10 new customers during Q2.

- Reduce production line downtime, due to maintenance, to less than 10% before the end of August.

- Reduce the time it takes to close the books at the end of the month from 9 to 6 working days as of March.

- Achieve a 15% market share for the new product within 6 months after the launch.

- Reduce inventory from 4.5 months to less than 3 months by the end of July.

At this point, your objectives should be clear and you should feel confident using them as an overall guide for what needs to be done.

If you are not confident about the WHAT, you may be easily swayed in different directions.

And your team may sway with you and not make any real progress. Worst of all, the team may become frustrated.

If you are unsure or easily swayed in different directions, you will tend to spin your wheels, rather than move forward. It is only when you feel confident that you have the WHAT right, that you can convey your passion and energy and get others to buy in.

The Team's What

Once you have established a clear objective for yourself—a clear WHAT—the time has come to align your team with it, if they have not already been involved in shaping the goal. By this point, you have sought input from various sources in the quest to crystalize your goal and you have perhaps even done some thinking about How you might get there.

As mentioned earlier, however, keep in mind that your team has not been on the same journey as you have. Even though you may have consulted the members of the team while formulating your goals, they were likely not exposed to the inputs you received from others in your network, including your manager and your peers. Consequently, you are in two very different places mentally. And, it is up to you, as the leader, to take your team members on the same journey you have been on so that they understand the trade-offs and how you ended up at the final destination—the WHAT.

Take a moment to reflect on how you got from "something needs to be done" to the point where you knew exactly WHAT needed to be done. How much have you already shared with your team? Did you share it with all members or just certain individuals? And, how big is the change?

To get buy-in, your first task is to help your team understand WHAT it is you want to achieve.

As the team starts to gain an understanding of the direction the project or task will take, the inevitable question that will arise is "Why?" Why is it important?

The answer to "Why?" can be found in the broader WHAT question: WHAT value will it add to the project, the business and the organization? For example, based on a couple of the goals outlined earlier in the section, the broader WHAT question could be answered as follows:

- By reducing our inventory from 4.5 months to 3 months or less, we can free up the money that is tied up in surplus inventory. Why?

Because there is a bigger WHAT behind this goal: We can then use that working capital to reduce our bank debt.

- If we can close our books at the end of the month in 6 days, rather than 9 days, we will know the results of the previous month sooner and, therefore, be in a better position to control the business. Again, there is a bigger WHAT behind this: A need to gain better control of the business.

In each case, the WHAT that you and your team aim to achieve fits into the organization's bigger WHAT. This underscores the importance of your piece of the bigger puzzle, i.e. how your objectives help support the bigger purpose and goals of the organization as a whole. (Later in the book, there will be more about breaking a complex target into manageable chunks and cascading them throughout the organization.)

Telling people about a good idea is not enough to ensure buy-in. Telling is a one-way form of communication. To get clarity and affect lasting change, you need to have multiple conversations from different angles over a period of time—it is an iterative process.

To achieve even deeper buy-in from team members, it may be worth involving them earlier in the process as discussed in the previous section. You may see a need to move in a certain direction, but you may not be able to work out the details in isolation because it is your team that has the detailed knowledge required to assess exactly how far you can go in that direction.

Involving the team fosters ownership. But even if you feel that your team has taken ownership of the WHAT, the selling never stops. The team's ownership of the goal is the key to its implementation.

Despite your best efforts, you may still sense that the team's picture of WHAT does not match your own. Or even worse, you sense the team is not motivated to achieve the desired results. As the leader, it is ultimately your job to drive results in the organization, so you need to assess the reasons for the lack of motivation before jumping into action. There are four possible causes:

1. **Your own view is vague.** If you are in doubt yourself on WHAT it is you want to achieve, the team's view will also be vague.

2. **The team misunderstands the WHAT.** The team does not fully understand the WHAT, its benefits and how it fits in with the organization's bigger WHAT—the bigger picture.

3. **The team disagrees with the WHAT.** There may be naysayers that do not see the value, or they may fear the consequences of the project, particularly if it involves efficiency gains. They may make you aware that they disagree, or even worse, they may disagree in silence.

4. **The team does not know How to move forward.** Some may feel frustrated by your expectations and by those team members who are capable of making progress. More on this topic in the next section.

If you sense resistance, the first step before you can resolve it is to understand the reasons for the resistance in the context of your actual situation. If it is a rather simple issue related to a misunderstanding, the solution could be more and better dialogue. Or, if the team is in direct disagreement with the WHAT, your solution will need to be different and it will need to address the specific issue. Most importantly, your response must address the specific underlying issue.

Ultimately, you want to come to the point where you and your team are aligned. A good indicator that there is buy-in amongst team members is when they start telling and selling the WHAT to others as their own. At this point, they have taken ownership of the project, and they are proud to be on board with their peers.

While the first part of the book has focused on the WHAT side of the model, the next part moves to the HOW side—turning WHAT into action.

How will you do it?

How encompasses the Competencies and Resources that will be required to achieve the What.

Once you have completed the foundation-laying aspect of leadership—created a clear vision or objective, described it in simple terms and taken the time to get people to buy-in—it is time to work on the How.

At this point, you could sit back and let the team work out a course of action, but this is exactly where leadership needs to step in. As a leader, you are responsible for not only the upfront work in establishing clear goals, but also making sure they are delivered, which is why it is critical that you take an active, yet balanced role, in getting there.

There is a big difference between orchestrating and doing. The leadership game is similar to a sports game: A coach cannot play the game; he or she can only lead from the sidelines. Viewing the game from sidelines rather than on the playing field provides a different perspective; it enables you to see the bigger picture and patterns of behaviour rather than focusing on actually playing. This offers excellent opportunities for giving advice and coaching the players. Likewise, leaders need to rely on the competencies and capabilities of others to achieve the goals, and they need to coach them from the sidelines. How many times have you thought that you could do it in half the time yourself? But, when you are in a leadership position, it is your job to motivate people and provide the support and training that will enable them to do a better job.

From the sidelines, leaders have the ability to view each team member's performance and evaluate areas where competencies need strengthening. The overview also allows leaders to see where additional resources are required, whether it is people, time or money (*refer to*

Figure 3). Indeed, it is these two areas that are critical components of How:

- **Competencies**. These include the different skills, abilities, knowledge and insights needed to do the tasks.

- **Resources.** These include people—the number of people across the various competencies required—as well as time and money.

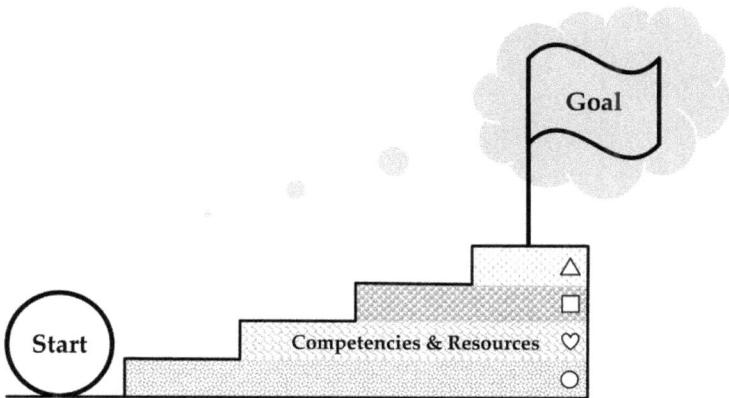

Figure 3: Reaching the goal requires the right mix of Competencies and Resources

When there is an imbalance between competencies and resources, you should not expect to see massive progress. Let us look at competencies and resources in more detail.

Competencies

To achieve your goals, your team needs certain competencies. Therefore, very conscious choices need to be made when assigning team members to a task or project. For example, you would not assign the chef in a kitchen to do the restaurant's books or a CEO to maintain the trucks, unless, by some luck of the draw, they happened to have competencies in those areas.

Competencies are seldom assessed on a day-to-day basis; instead, this task is often saved for the annual or bi-annual performance review. At the start of a major new project or new way of doing business, a crucial first step is to understand the kinds of competencies required for the task. It may be easy to look at the existing organization and appoint "the usual suspects," but by starting with a clean slate, and defining the types of competencies needed, you are taking the first step towards ensuring that you will assign people with the right level of absolute competencies rather than the ones available.

Say you own a shop, and you want to start selling your products on the Internet. There may be someone on your team who knows a lot about computers and the Internet, so they may seem like the obvious choice to build your e-commerce site.

But before approaching your colleague, take a moment to consider what skills are required to build an e-commerce site, e.g. experience with security matters, payments, inventory and accounting integration, etc. Your colleague's interest, passion and qualifications might be in the right direction. But does he or she have all of the skills required?

You need to first determine the key skills that are required to do the task, and then consider whether your team member is the right choice. It is only when you have defined the absolute requirements that you can then compare the team member's skills with the requirements to determine whether there is a match.

You may have team members who are performing well today, but after reflecting on the absolute set of skills required for an upcoming task or project, you realize that their qualifications need to be strengthened in certain areas. And eventually, through an open dialogue about upcoming requirements, you realize that your team members actually possess skills or talents that you were not aware of initially.

A lack of competencies in the team is not necessarily a bad sign. It is an indicator that your WHAT is ambitious enough to challenge the status quo. And, your newfound awareness of the competencies that need strengthening will provide opportunities for development. Without going through the exercise of assessing competencies, the project may end up stalling due to a lack of competencies. Now that you are aware of the competency gap, you can act on it.

How do you handle competency gaps?

Fire people and hire new ones? Hire consultants? Send everyone on a training course? The answer of course depends; it may be none of the above, some combination of the above or something completely different. There is no universal answer; it will depend on your situation.

Ultimately, leaders need to ensure that the right competencies are available at the right time. And yes, consultants, new people, interim solutions and other non-evolutionary approaches are sometimes the right option for large, complex tasks or projects.

However, in most cases—which is our focus in LEADERSHIP: LESSON ONE—you will probably work with an existing team, where certain competencies need to be strengthened. In this respect, the good news is that most people have not reached their full potential. That is, they are capable of developing new competencies. And true leaders are committed to helping people come closer to reaching their full potential. In doing so, they send a strong message to their teams that they have confidence in them and see development of people as a natural and integrated enabler for growing the business.

In the example about building e-commerce for your store, your team member may have most of the required competencies, except for online payment and accounting integration. Recognizing this gap in competencies offers an excellent opportunity to learn and grow, to the benefit of both the team member and your store. But first, it needs to be recognized and addressed.

Leaders play a crucial role in expanding the capabilities of the team. Rather than doing the training themselves, they play a significant role in shaping the developmental path. To embark on this road, the leader needs to communicate the need for change and improvement and be patient with the gradual growth in competence among team members.

While an individual's development may include some training, the strongest source of growth comes from challenging people beyond their comfort zones during day-to-day work. This is where the leader can play a major role, pushing people beyond their comfort zones, while standing by, offering support, and coaching when needed. As the leader, you shoulder responsibility for doing everything you can to help them succeed. When successful, the employee will feel energized and more confident.

Helping people grow into their potential is one of the biggest and most rewarding accomplishments you, as a leader, can make.

In some cases, the employee may falter under the weight of the challenge. Most people know when they have failed or made a mistake in a situation. Depending on how the situation is handled, the person will either feel guilty or grow as a result. For a leader, this type of situation can be a gold mine for learning, provided the leader can create an environment in which constructive feedback is perceived not as criticism but as a source of empowerment.

How do you handle mistakes in your organization? Do they provoke a feeling of guilt, or are they discussed openly and used as learning opportunities?

Questions like the following will help turn these situations into learning opportunities rather than guilt-ridden exchanges: What did you learn? What would you do differently next time? What support do you need? Etc.

Much in the same way that professional athletes improve, you can develop your team members by helping them learn from their mistakes, adjust their behaviours, try out new things, stretch their comfort zones and continuously improve until they reach the high-performance level that will give them a leading edge.

Once you are sure you have the right competencies on board, you need to bring them into play and ensure they cooperate. Your restaurant can have the best chef and a world-class waiter, but unless they cooperate and interact, the guest experience will not reflect the world-class staff that you have recruited.

Competencies and cooperation go hand in hand: If you had the best chef, but only a second-class waiter, they would not be able to deliver a world-class experience even if they cooperated. The end result is only as good as the leader's ability to bring together the people with the right competencies and ensure that they cooperate with one another.

There is no progress without both competencies and cooperation. And there is no growth in competencies and cooperation without your leadership support.

Resources

In addition to competencies, it takes resources to make progress. If all of your competent employees are busy doing other things, you cannot make progress. Progress requires the right balance between competencies and resources.

There is a broad variety of resources, including the number of people involved, the time they spend on the task or project and, if relevant, the money invested in the task. With the right balance among people, time and money, you gain traction and with it, progress.

The total time span it takes to finish a task or project is also a resource that should be included in the equation. Change takes time. Deciding between fast-paced, bold change and gradual change over a longer time span can be a delicate balancing act. Expecting massive changes in too short a period may be over-optimistic; yet, by extending it over too long a timeframe, you risk having the energy seep out of the project.

In the leadership role, your decisions and adjustments regarding time, money and people are the very foundation for success.

In some cases, when too little progress is being made, extra resources are often the obvious and easy solution—more money, additional IT support, more finance staff, etc. But, before you decide that you need more resources, take a moment to reflect on exactly how those resources can move your project forward.

Do you need more time? Because the learning is taking longer than anticipated or the solution is more complex than you initially thought? Or, will more heads and hands, new tools or money make a difference?

You need to be clear about exactly what kinds of resources are needed because this links back to competencies.

Additional resources may also be a high priority for your team members, particularly if the majority of their work is non-project related, and their day-to-day tasks are taking most of their time and energy, leaving little left over for project work. Rather than pumping more resources into the project, you might consider ways to move the project to the top of their agendas. This may require selling their managers on the WHAT, or asking that they be released from other duties for the duration of the project. A small number of team members dedicated solely to the project can often have a bigger impact than a large project team, where each member only has a small portion of time to spend on the project.

Rather than adding additional people resources to the project, which means more coordination, administration, complexity and expense, you can challenge the team to come up with a more creative approach. The 1970 Apollo 13 voyage is a great example of this: The famous quote, "Houston we've had a problem here" during the Apollo 13 flight energized an amazing and life-saving level of creativity. Cube shaped canisters with an air-cleaning agent needed to fit into cylindrical canister sockets. Square boxes into round holes! Without a solution, the astronauts would die from a lack of oxygen.

In the control centre in Houston, the team gathered replicas of every available piece of material on board the Apollo 13, put it all on a table with a clear objective—the WHAT: Create a solution that could be replicated on board the Apollo spacecraft that was flying around in outer space.

The Apollo spacecraft crew simply could not ask for more resources, but a clear WHAT (deliver a solution!) inspired a lot of creative energy. And as featured in the movie *Apollo 13*, they reached a solution that actually did save the lives of the astronauts. The only extra resource was creativity.

In some cases, creativity can be better than extra resources. And on top of that, it can be more fun breaking down the barriers that surround "the normal way of doing things."

How could a more creative approach move your project forward, given your current resources?

The What-How Ecosystem

In the previous section, we discussed WHAT and HOW in detail. But, in reality, the world is a little more complex. The leadership role is often summed up in terms of defining the strategic direction and objectives and setting targets and goals—the WHAT piece of the leadership puzzle. As for the HOW piece, you, as the leader, are ultimately responsible for acquiring the necessary resources and ensuring that your team has developed the competencies required to meet the objectives and satisfy the stakeholders. We describe the combination of these actions as the WHAT–HOW Ecosystem (*refer to **Figure 4***).

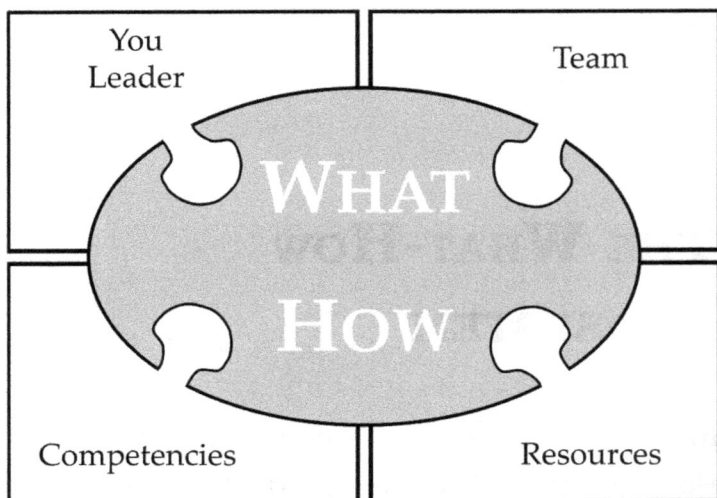

Figure 4: The WHAT-HOW Ecosystem

The WHAT–HOW Ecosystem consists of four components—Leader and Team are connected to WHAT, and Competencies and Resources are connected to HOW—all of which are connected to one another similar to a biological ecosystem. For example, take a plant in your living room; it requires the right mix of soil, sun, air, water and temperature. Like the WHAT–HOW Ecosystem, if one component is out of sync, it is difficult to compensate with another, e.g. without water, a plant cannot benefit from more sun.

While each of the four components in **Figure 4** is an important part of the Ecosystem, finding the right balance is equally important. Rather than waiting for the annual or bi-annual strategy review or performance review, it is essential that leaders continuously assess the need for rebalancing their unique ecosystems.

This simple, yet powerful approach is at the core of leadership, and it is universally applicable. If you are embarking on a new challenge, get it on track by determining the right balance among these four components to achieve the results you desire. But do not stop there; frequently reassess and adjust as often as required to stay on track.

If you already have a task or project on the go and it is not progressing as you wish, go back to this simple framework and re-examine the four components—this is where you will find the root cause of your lack of progress.

Motivation and Leading Edge performance

When the WHAT is fully understood by you and your team, there may be a need to support the HOW. For example, say a junior team member is fully capable of doing the easier stuff—the HOW—on a small project, but gets swept off track with creative thinking; he or she may need to be reminded of the destination—the WHAT—in a bit more detail, to make sure his or her energy and creativity are headed in the right direction—towards the WHAT (*refer to* **Figure 5**).

It is like trying to balance on an unstable surface; you constantly need to work one side and then the other—and it never stops.

WHAT
is your goal

HOW
you achieve it

Figure 5: Constantly ensure that HOW is feeding into WHAT

In any project or task, there is always something that can be done better, or could have been done better. This applies not only to your team, but also to you, your behaviour, your learning journey and your leadership style.

With the right leadership and a new task or project, you can push the boundaries of your team to help it grow, continuously improving its capabilities and enabling it to make an even bigger difference next time. Ultimately, you want to reach a position where the team's way of working is leading edge, and that eventually the right team members become qualified to take on even bigger responsibilities.

If you sign up for helping your team grow its competencies, you will get the additional benefit of growing your own leadership skills because the task of growing team competencies requires good leadership.

Doing things without understanding WHAT the ultimate goal is makes little sense to anyone. When your team members buy in to the purpose of the task, they have an understanding of its importance and they will be motivated to contribute to its success (*refer to* **Figure 6**). It is this clear understanding of WHAT that generates the energy to contribute in a meaningful way. When the objective is unclear, it is hard to get motivated.

If we look at sports, we see that motivation is important, but motivation is not the only factor for the greatest athletes. It is the dream of winning or achieving great results that motivates them to reach the leading edge of their sport. This constant focus on winning motivates athletes to train for hours and work on continually improving their performance—the HOW.

Motivation   HOW
you achieve it

WHAT   Leading Edge
is your goal

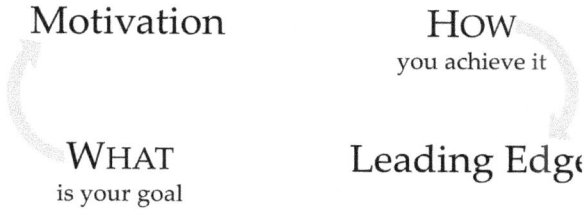

*Figure 6: WHAT drives motivation, HOW provides
leading edge performance*

However, the same training over and over
again will not produce leading-edge results.
Instead, athletes need to constantly seek ways
to optimize their performance by making small
improvements and seeking new ways of doing
things.

The parallel to leadership is the importance of
leaders creating an environment that encourages
new and better ways of doing things—not just
for the team but also for themselves. When you
challenge yourself and your team to stretch
beyond the comfort zone, competencies will
increase. By repeating this process, you create
a virtuous circle of continuously increasing
competencies (*refer to **Figure 7***).

Motivation

WHAT
is your goal

HOW
you achieve it

Leading Edge

*Figure 7: WHAT drives motivation, HOW provides
leading edge performance*

Leading edge does not just refer to patents, products or unique services. Individuals and teams can also possess leading-edge competencies in the way they work, the processes they follow, the way they cooperate within their organizations, how they lead and manage projects, the way they deliver customer service, etc. But it is a clear WHAT that drives the motivation to train for the HOW and the more you train the closer you come to being leading edge.

Cascading Goals

In 1961, with his famous words, "We choose to go to the Moon in this decade ...," U.S. President John F. Kennedy stated a very clear WHAT!

Under this giant WHAT, a large number of Hows evolved, including building a spacecraft, training astronauts, calculating the ideal flying and landing schedule, developing food supplies for the journey, etc.

If we zoom in closer, and focus on the engineers building the spacecraft that would take people to the Moon and back, we see that this in itself was an objective—a WHAT. For those engineers, the one and only task on their plates was to build the spacecraft—their specific WHAT. And their WHAT was one of the Hows in the bigger picture.

Zooming in even closer on the spacecraft project, we see that the engineers had to figure out all of the Hows, including landing and take-off design for the lunar capsule, fresh air supply throughout the journey, space suits for walking on the Moon, etc. And again, the objective of creating a space suit for walking on the moon was in itself a new WHAT for the team of specialists who had to figure out all the Hows associated with that piece of the project.

WHAT and How are the two key words all the way from the vision and the organization's reason to exist right down to every member of the organization.

The organization's mission or reason to exist is the ultimate WHAT.

This is often broken down into strategic pillars, i.e. How to deliver the mission. Each strategic pillar becomes a new WHAT, e.g. "10% of our turnover is to come from innovations launched within the last 12 months." In order to make sense of each pillar, they need to be broken down into new Hows.

The hierarchy is not only a picture of the vision, strategy and projects in an organization; it also reflects projects or tasks with an overall objective—the WHAT. In this project, there may be milestones to achieve, which are the WHATS on the second level, and within each of these milestones, there may be assignments to sub-teams or team members, who are assigned the WHAT on the third level (*refer to* **Figure 8**).

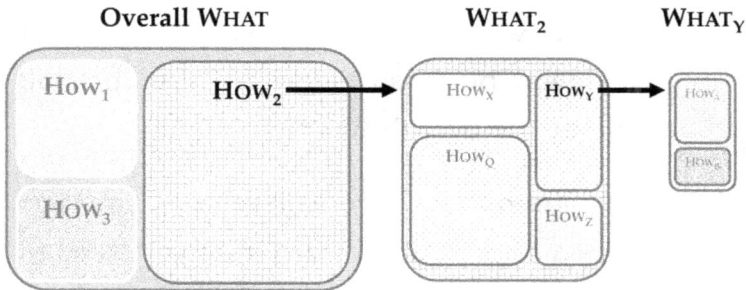

Figure 8: Breaking down WHAT and HOW

The hierarchy works on a macro level starting with a vision at the top—WHAT we strive for as an organization. And it continues all the way down to the lowest level of the organization.

In an ideal state, the Whats and Hows from the highest level through to the lowest level are aligned, and they all feed into the overall objectives of the organization.

Are these layers aligned in your organization? Do you see the Whats turning into Hows all the way from your organization's overall vision down to your own role and the tasks and project(s) you are currently leading?

Are the layers integrated, i.e. are they inter-related in a way that makes sense—not just up and down, but also sideways? Do they all complement the overall What?

Do the Whats on the second level feed into the overall What on the first level? Or do you need to clarify the What of some of your projects to make them contribute more directly to the overall What?

Or, even worse, is the work being done at one level not delivering against the ultimate What?

Vision, strategy, project names and job descriptions are the banners under which we find the small, yet important, print—the words that shape the actions of the company.

In addition to facilitating integration between each level, the hierarchy model also fosters transparency on how well the work taking place at the lower levels is contributing to the overall objective of the project or organization—the ultimate WHAT, and as discussed earlier, this is a key driver of motivation.

WHAT and HOW are closely inter-related; they integrate the overall corporate goals with the actions required to deliver them. That process implies breaking the high-level WHATs formulated as strategic initiatives and major projects, or whatever you call them, into meaningful HOWs. These more meaningful HOWs need to be broken down again into even more meaningful and specific activities—that is breaking the Hows into WHATs and cascading them throughout the organization.

This shows everyone in the organization how their daily actions, tasks and projects contribute to the overall success of the organization and ensures that resources are aligned with strategic priorities.

Two Types of Leaders: What & How

There are many paths one can follow into a leadership role, but there are two paths that generally lead in that direction: Either you were a functional expert in your field or you have a strong ability to energize people to deliver on highly visual and well-communicated targets.

If you were a functional expert, with strong capabilities that were recognized by management before you were promoted, you are a How leader. You are still an expert in the area of your responsibility, but you probably feel a little overwhelmed about your new role even though you are confident about your expertise.

If you were the team member with an ability to motivate people, you are probably an opinion leader amongst your colleagues and spend a lot of time influencing and energizing others. You probably do not know the details of what your team members do, but you always make sure that they know the goal and direction. You are a WHAT leader, and you constantly keep your eye on the target.

Both types of leaders have strong capabilities and strengths, yet in different areas.

The HOW leader's expertise allows him or her to support the team's progress. The WHAT leader's team knows exactly what it has to achieve and where it is headed, but it may not always get the operational support it needs.

Knowing where to go—what the goal looks like—is great, but only if the support on HOW to get there is available. This ensures that the team not only achieves the goal in a quality way, but also, more importantly, makes sure the team members' capabilities increase as they make their way towards the objective.

And vice versa, a How leader, can provide a lot of support and improve the teams' skills. But if the overall objective, the vision for the end result, is not clear and motivating, there is the risk that the team will end up spinning its wheels rather than moving towards the What.

While both types of leaders have a lot to contribute, they also have a lot of room for development—the fields are different, but they are equally important.

The functional expert—the How leader—can develop his or her ability to better shape the What and sell it.

And the What leader can enhance progress by offering support to team members that will enable them to improve their skill level in order to reach the What.

The perfect leader may exist, i.e. one who is equally capable in both the What and How arenas. But both types of leaders, regardless of their type, along with their teams, have the ability to continue to grow and increase their capabilities. A one-off seminar or leadership program will not do the trick; it requires daily persistence and energy to challenge your abilities. There is no quick fix for this.

Take a moment to reflect on your own style.

Do you see yourself in one of the columns, and can you identify a colleague or peer in the other?

We often tend to seek inspiration from people that are similar to us. Try to think of someone who is successful, but has a very different style from you. What elements in her or his style could inspire you?

	What Leader	**How Leader**
Reason for first promotion	Strong influencer, strong focus on targets.	Strong functional competencies and skills.
Typical strengths	Articulates strong What, sets targets and direction. Energizing direction-setter.	Expertise, knowledge and experience. Functional expert.
Typical development areas	Patience to see people grow and develop as a pre-requisite for making sustainable results. Continuous assessment and development of competencies and resources.	Articulate a strong What, and energize the team to run for success. Leave progress to the team; refrain from instructing in too much detail.

TAKE A LOOK IN THE MIRROR

LEADERSHIP: LESSON ONE is intended to be an asset for you, something useful that can help you in your leadership role, no matter your level of experience.

In order to get the most from this simple, yet powerful framework, you have to work with it. This is where your fun really begins, and where your reflection should lead to learning that will ultimately help make you more successful in your leadership role.

You can choose to read this section once and move on like you would with most books. You will probably find that it is a quick read, but to get the most out of it, you need to take some time to reflect on it.

By reflecting on the questions in this section, your own continuous learning journey begins. Once you have time to think about what you have read, consider reading it again because you will pick up on new things each time you do.

Let the reflection begin!

Take a moment to think about a recent or, even better, a current project or task. Ideally, it is a task or project where you would like to see more or better progress than what you are currently seeing. It must be a task or project that you are deeply involved in and ideally responsible for, or one where you can at least influence the progress by taking a lead in some direction. It may be progressing too slowly or not at all. Perhaps the quality is poor, the impact is not up to par or the team's behaviour has deteriorated, and it is not making enough progress or it is at a standstill.

Do you have a project or task in mind?

Congratulations! You have passed the first important hurdle. You have been honest with yourself, and you now have your focus on something within your responsibility that you would like to improve. And remember, at this point, only you are aware that you have started thinking about this.

Now that you have identified the problem, the first step is to figure out if the lack of progress is caused by issues relating to WHAT or HOW—or a combination of both. To do this, try answering the following questions:

1. What is the goal of the task or project? Where do you want it to go? What does success look like? What criteria are you using to define success?

   The critical element here is to shape a picture in your own mind of what success really looks like; what the dream is all about. Is your definition of your goal only a milestone in a bigger project? For example, if your goal is to have a new product launched by September or a new machine or website installed by

May, ask yourself if launching a product or installing a machine is the ultimate goal. Or, is there a bigger corporate goal, e.g. sell 30,000 pieces of the new product by the end of the year. If that is the case, then a September 1 launch or installing a new machine or website are only milestones that need to be achieved in order to sell 30,000 pieces by the end of the year.

Once you are confident with your version of WHAT, move on. If you are not ready, leave it for a day or two, then come back and read it again. Usually the answers do not come all at once.

2. If you talk to the most important players on the team, how would they explain the purpose, goal, aim of the project to their friends or other colleagues? How would they explain what they are working on?

You may actually want to do a little field research, and check in with them over the coming days in order to understand if they actually share the exact same vision of the goal as you do. Are they describing it in the same way as you are—the same timing, same amounts, same quality or however you have articulated the picture of success?

If their version of the end goal is not the same as yours, perhaps the goal lacks some clearly stated targets in terms of time, money, etc. This calls for action from your side in order to calibrate expectations.

When everyone's vision of the task or project—the What—is aligned, you can then concentrate on How. Until that happens, you need to work on bringing everyone to the same point in terms of a shared objective— the What.

Once you and your team are aligned on What your objective is, move on to How.

3. How will you get there? How much progress has been made? How will the team get there? What is actually happening on the task or project? During this stage, your thinking needs to be practical: Physically, what is happening, what activities are being carried out—or not? Are the actions moving you closer to the target, or is the team spinning its wheels and not moving forward. Most importantly, what is the reason for the

lack of progress? Does it relate to a lack of competencies or poor cooperation between different people with different competencies, or is it related to resources—time, money, creativity?

Try to be as specific as possible, e.g. person X is not contributing, person Y is delivering poor quality, they are all talk and no action, T and Q are not cooperating, etc. Do you see issues related to competencies or resources—or both? In that case, this can be a likely reason for the lack of progress (*refer to **Figure 9***).

Hopefully, you have now reached the first important conclusion—something is wrong. Thanks to asking the right questions and your reflection, or your talks with the team or others, it has helped you get to the root cause of the issue and now you are ready to take action to resolve it.

No matter where you see the issue, you have recognized it, which is the ultimate foundation for deciding what actions to take in both the WHAT and HOW domains.

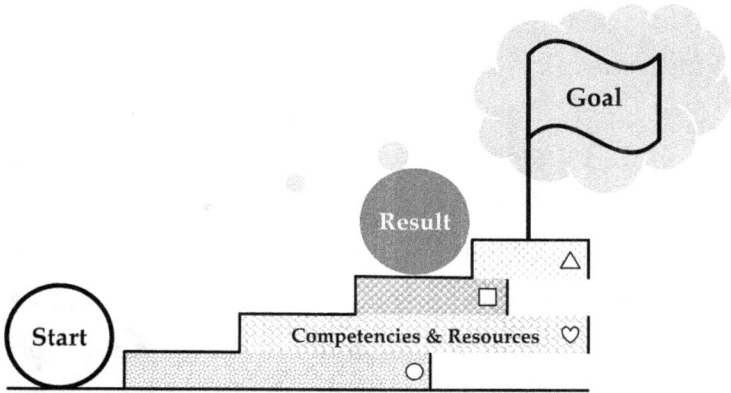

Figure 9: Results can suffer if competencies and/or resources are lacking.

Recognizing that something is wrong is a great achievement! It is now up to you to get the progress back on track. It is also time to reflect on your own behaviour in terms of leadership. Did you notice patterns in your behaviour that could be changed to help the team move on? For example, have you been too focused on How before making sure that What is clearly anchored? Or have you been so focused on What it is you have to deliver, that you have not picked up on signals from the team that it needs support on How to improve progress. This is not to suggest that you should do the teams' job for them; instead, some coaching and an open dialogue might help them get over a hurdle.

Another insightful exercise is to think back in time—two days, weeks or months depending on the scale of your task. If you could have done something differently, what would it be? And if you had done it differently, where would you be today? And, most importantly, what did this little exercise teach you to be aware of going forward?

While this exercise of looking in the mirror may sometimes be a little painful, it is beneficial if you can transform the new insights you gain into positive actions that enable you and the team to grow and move forward.

And ... action!

Every new challenge or task comes with a learning curve. Undoubtedly, there will be some bumps along the way. And the fear of failure may loom large. But to limit the psychological hit from failing, you need to start viewing failure as non-terminal, and instead, see it for what it is—a learning experience. As Bill Gates once said, "Success is a lousy teacher. It seduces smart people into thinking they can't lose."

Do not fear seeking advice from your manager, team, peers or your friends. By asking, you send a strong signal that you care. You want to improve. And, you are open to input.

Most people love to help. Then, it is up to you to consider their advice, decide what makes sense and use it to the max.

It is my hope that this book will give leaders a good send off to any new endeavour. My advice: Practice, take action, make some mistakes and, most importantly, learn along the way. And check back from time to time to keep the simple model from LEADERSHIP: LESSON ONE fresh in your mind as you continue on your leadership journey.

**The journey of a thousand miles
begins with a single step.**

Lao Tzu

APPENDIX

I am by no means a big fan of filling in grids and templates for the sake of filling them in. In some cases, however, a template can help organize your thinking because it provides a very structured framework for going through a sequence step-by-step and considering each step along the way.

Therefore, as a starting point, it may be worth filling in the following charts because they will help you actively work with the framework and force you to consider all of the relevant aspects.

OVERVIEW OF THE FOUR COMPONENTS IN THE WHAT-HOW ECOSYSTEM

My WHAT	Goal
_____	
_____	
_____	
_____	

Teams' WHAT	Goal
☹	☺
Ms. X _____	
Mr. Y _____	
Mrs Z _____	
Mr. A _____	

Competencies □ △ ○ ♡

△ _____

♡ _____

□ _____

○ _____

Resources □ △ ○ ♡

1   10

△ ◁◁◁◁◁◀

♡ ◁◁◁◁◁◀

□ ◁◁◁◁◁◀

○ ◁◁◁◁◁◀

EXAMPLE OF A COMPLETED OVERVIEW

My WHAT	Goal

Achieve XYZ

performance by Nov 20XZ

_____

_____

Teams' WHAT	Goal

😕   🙂

Ms. X   x

Mr. Y   x

Mrs Z   x

Mr. A   **x**

Competencies □ △ ○ ♡

△   Crazy ideas

♡   Admin support

□   Financial skills

○   Webshop skills

Resources □ △ ○ ♡

          1   10

△   [X]

♡   [X]

□   [X]

○   [X]

Root Cause Maze

When things do not go as one wishes, it is a natural instinct to want to fix it—the sooner the better.

But before running off to fix something, make sure you are fixing the right problem. It may seem obvious that you need to water a plant with brown leaves. But if the real problem is a lack of sunlight, water alone will not help.

The following "maze" is a sequential guide to help you find the root cause of a lack of progress:

Lack of progress: Symptom checker

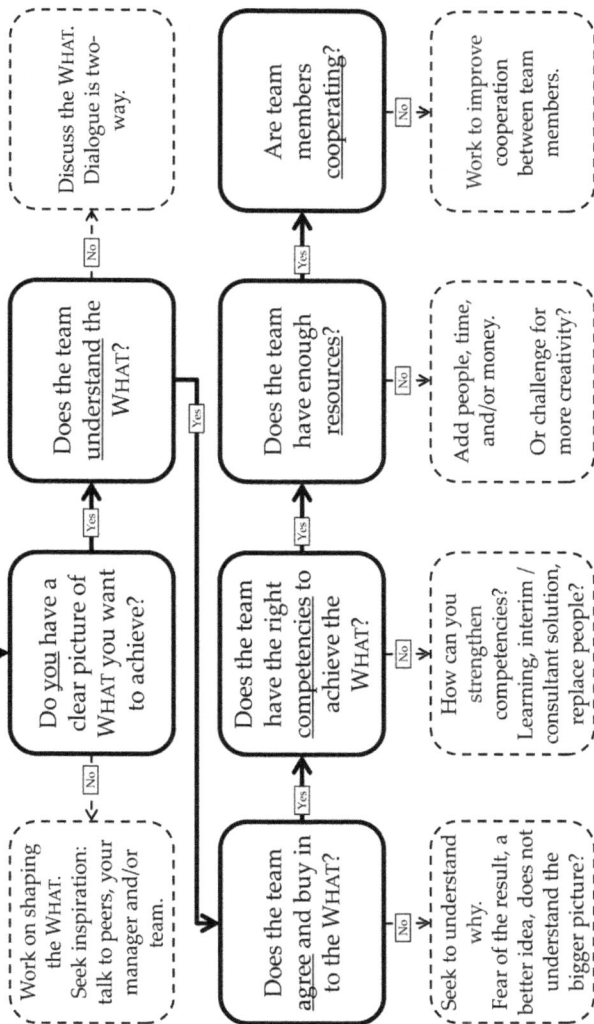

Do you have a clear picture of WHAT you want to achieve?

- No → *Work on shaping the WHAT. Seek inspiration: talk to peers, your manager and/or team.*
- Yes → **Does the team understand the WHAT?**
  - No → *Discuss the WHAT. Dialogue is two-way.*
  - Yes → **Does the team agree and buy in to the WHAT?**
    - No → *Seek to understand why. Fear of the result, a better idea, does not understand the bigger picture?*
    - Yes → **Does the team have the right competencies to achieve the WHAT?**
      - No → *How can you strengthen competencies? Learning, interim / consultant solution, replace people?*
      - Yes → **Does the team have enough resources?**
        - No → *Add people, time, and/or money. Or challenge for more creativity?*
        - Yes → **Are team members cooperating?**
          - No → *Work to improve cooperation between team members.*

ACKNOWLEDGEMENTS

I have had the fortune of working with many skilled people over the years from whom I have learned a lot. And probably like most others, I can identify a handful of people who have had a major impact in shaping who I am professionally. I owe a big thanks to two people in particular: Jan Sterobo and Nick Dieltiens.

Jan only hired me once, but we happened to work together in three different companies. As my manager for a total of more than 12 years, he gave me confidence and helped me develop from the basics in marketing many years ago into a multi-national business leader several years later.

As the founder, mastermind, and the first VP of the Continuous Improvement community at

Sara Lee Europe, Nick not only gave me a whole new Lean toolbox, but also offered an inspiring, holistic and very useful way of structured thinking, applicable in both business and life.

A big thanks for input at various stages throughout the development of this book and for encouraging comments along the way to Mette Madsen, Lise Moeller, Lene Skyttegaard Bach, Torben Hedegaard Nielsen, and Hanne Buje Jensen. And a special thanks to Lars Carlsen and Peter Møhring for the inspiring talks, your valueable input and the exchange of ideas.

During the finalization, I enjoyed working with Beverley Lennox: You did a fantastic job on editing, and in challenging my words and sentences in a very constructive way. Mila Perry came up with the great idea for the cover design and the symbol of the flying birds, and was faster than fast in the final rounds of small but important adjustments.

Thanks, too, to my Dad. The wise comments and questions, also to this project, are always appreciated.

And without the support from Dorthe, Caroline and Christian, I would neither have had the courage nor the freedom to pursue this dream. Thanks for your support and patience with me!

ABOUT THE AUTHOR

Morten Heedegaard has worked for more than 25 years in several international companies across different industries. He has accumulated 15 years of leadership experience in various positions.

His experience includes leading commercial sales and marketing operations across more than 15 European countries, several years on the management team of a multi-country consumer goods company, and extensive functional experience in marketing, sales, export management and customer partnering and development.

He has been leading and facilitating projects up to a European scale within the areas of sales, marketing, innovation, finance and supply chain, aiming to grow both customer satisfaction and company results.

Morten speaks, presents and facilitates with passion and energy, and he is appreciated for his ability to orchestrate projects and workshops that range from operational who-does-what-how workshops to multi-day management team sessions.

He believes in bringing out the best in people, and that continuous development of people, tools and processes is a prerequisite for an organization's continuous success.

NOTES

NOTES